Etiquette for Success
Social Media & Online Manners

TITLES IN THE SERIES

Etiquette for Success
Social Media & Online Manners

Sarah Smith

MASON CREST

Mason Crest
450 Parkway Drive, Suite D
Broomall, Pennsylvania PA 19008
(866) MCP-BOOK (toll free)

First printing
9 8 7 6 5 4 3 2 1

ISBN: 978-1-4222-3973-5
Series ISBN: 978-1-4222-3969-8
ebook ISBN: 978-1-4222-7812-3

Cataloging-in-Publication Data on file with the Library of Congress.

Printed and bound in the United States of America.

QR CODES AND LINKS TO THIRD-PARTY CONTENT

Contents

KEY ICONS TO LOOK FOR:

Words to Understand: These words with their easy-to-understand definitions will increase the reader's understanding of the text while building vocabulary skills.

Sidebars: This boxed material within the main text allows readers to build knowledge, gain insights, explore possibilities, and broaden their perspectives by weaving together additional information to provide realistic and holistic perspectives.

Educational Videos: Readers can view videos by scanning our QR codes, providing them with additional content to supplement the text. Examples include news coverage, moments in history, speeches, iconic sports moments, and much more!

Text-Dependent Questions: These questions send the reader back to the text for more careful attention to the evidence presented there.

Research Projects: Readers are pointed toward areas of further inquiry connected to each chapter. Suggestions are provided for projects that encourage deeper research and analysis.

Series Glossary of Key Terms: This back-of-the-book glossary contains terminology used throughout the series. Words found here increase the reader's ability to read and comprehend higher-level books and articles in this field.

Dear Reader,

As you read on, you will learn that in any given situation you must be knowledgeable about the expectations set by society regarding your actions and how they will or will not meet the social norms for good manners and etiquette.

It being essential to your success, you learn how your behavior will always be central to how others see you. Unfortunately, many people are judged, or written off almost instantly because of their lack of etiquette.

Times have certainly changed, and while society adapts, you must set your own goals for politeness, good manners, and kindness. All around you there are modern dilemmas to face, but let your good manners set you apart. Start by showing sensitivity toward others, maintain a keen awareness about how those around you feel, and note how your behavior impacts your peers.

Consider that even with changes in the world around you, etiquette must be inclusive and understanding across ages and cultures, and sensitive to your setting. It is important that you take the time to learn; read, practice, and ask questions of those whom you respect. Learn about writing a business letter, sending holiday invitations, or communicating with peers— certain etiquettes should be followed. Is it rude to keep checking your phone during lunch with a friend? Are handwritten thank-you notes still necessary?

It is said that good manners open doors that even the best education cannot. Read on and learn what it takes to make a great first impression.

"No duty is more urgent than that of returning thanks."

"No matter who you are or what you do, your manners will have a direct impact on your professional and social success."

"Respect for ourselves guides our morals; respect for others guides our manners"

"Life is short, but there is always time enough for courtesy"

Words to Understand

appropriate: suitable or fitting for a particular purpose, person, or occasion

considerate: careful not to cause inconvenience or hurt to others

etiquette: the customary code of polite behavior among members of a particular society, profession, or group

Social media is a way of life for teens and adults alike. However, to stay safe online, it is important to understand some important rules that will enable you to make the most of the good sites currently available.

Chapter One
The Importance of
Good Online Etiquette

Everybody enjoys being appreciated and respected. As a teenager, your ability to present yourself in a positive way will have a dramatic impact on the way others see you. In other words, if you want to be respected, be respectful. If you want to be treated fairly, treat others fairly. *Do unto others as you would have others do unto you.* This is the Golden Rule —no wonder it has been around for centuries!

Most of us spend a lot of time on our phones, tablets, and computers. Of course, this isn't necessarily a bad thing. Our modern digital age has made it easier to find information about the world we're living in. The growing online community has also helped us connect with other people on a much larger scale. This allows us to develop personal and professional relationships with others in a way that people from generations ago never could have done.

How Often Are You Online?
According to data collected by the nonprofit organization Common Sense Media, the average teen spends about 6 hours per day using digital screen media, which includes things like Facebook, YouTube, Instagram, and online games.

Presenting yourself in a positive way online can be particularly tricky. Why? Because on the internet, we can't use body language, tone of voice, and facial expressions to interact with others. These forms of *nonverbal communication* are an essential part of human language and have developed over thousands of years. Without them, it can be difficult to understand someone (or for someone to understand you).

Think about it: have you ever sent a text, tweet, Facebook post, or email that somebody else thought was rude? Were you shocked or embarrassed to learn that someone thought you were trying to be mean, even if you weren't?

Saying or doing something you wish you hadn't is one thing; posting it online where everyone can see it is another—and it comes with many unique consequences.

This is why it's so important to develop good online etiquette. After all, it's not always possible to control how others will respond to something you do or say. But it is possible to develop smarter habits that will help you communicate more effectively online and maximize the safety and well-being of yourself and others.

The Importance of Good Online Etiquette

What Is Good Etiquette, Anyway?

Good **etiquette** is such a crucial yet often overlooked skill. It's not something you're born with. It's something that you learn over time. Parents, teachers, religious leaders, coaches, friends, and even characters from books, TV shows, and movies can all be models that teach us how to behave in a polite and socially acceptable way.

Of course, practicing good etiquette means a lot more than just having good posture and saying "please" and "thank you." A person with good etiquette is generally seen in a positive light by others. He or she is the type of person that others like being around. He or she can be expected to enjoy higher quality relationships, both personally and professionally.

Specifically, a person with great etiquette is **considerate**, honest, tactful, gracious, generous, and fair. These and other qualities of good etiquette are important not just in your day-to-day world, but in your online world as well.

Respect and good manners are just as important online as well as in the real world.

What to Expect From This Book

The purpose of this book is to teach you what good etiquette looks like online and how to develop it yourself. Relevant words will be defined to help expand your knowledge, and questions and exercises at the end of each chapter will help you apply what you've learned. Doing them will help give you the confidence to start using your online etiquette in a practical everyday way.

Your introduction to online etiquette will begin with learning about the best ways to use social media platforms like Facebook, Twitter, Snapchat, and Instagram. You'll also learn about online safety and why personal information should be kept private.

Today we live in a virtual world as well as a real one. Everyday, we are bombarded with prods, tweets, messages, and friend requests. It is vital to be able to know when to respond and when not to.

You'll also learn how to improve your email etiquette. This includes coming up with a respectful email address and knowing when email is **appropriate** to use (and when it's not).

Cyberbullying, "trolling," and other harmful online behaviors are important topics to cover for improving your online etiquette. You'll learn how to protect yourself from online harassment, what to do if you think someone you know is instigating online bullying, and how to treat everyone you meet online in a more respectful way.

You'll also learn how to find authoritative internet resources. This can help you with school projects or simply help you advance your own understanding of current affairs around the world.

The Importance of Good Online Etiquette

Use the time you spend online in a positive way, remembering that almost every site you log on to leaves a "digital footprint."

Good etiquette online can make a big difference for your future academic and professional careers. You'll learn the tactful art of self-promotion and the ins and outs of business networks like LinkedIn. Making and retaining good contacts with potential employers, mentors, and peers is key. You'll also learn why almost everything you do online leaves a "digital footprint" that can have either a positive or negative impact on your future.

Lastly, you'll be provided with a list of recommended readings so you can further your understanding of online etiquette as it applies to all the different ways you use the internet every day.

So, let's log on and begin!

Text-Dependent Questions

1. How long does the average teen spend on digital screen media each day?

2. Why is good etiquette a crucial skill?

3. How do people with good etiquette tend to be seen by others?

Research Project

Write an essay on how good etiquette and good manners can help you achieve your goals in life. Then, using the internet, research eight golden rules of good online etiquette and manners.

Words to Understand

app: short for application, or a piece of software that is typically downloadable onto a computer, tablet, or phone and used to perform a specific function or task

social media: a way to digitally share information and communicate with others quickly. Typically through social media websites or platforms like Facebook, Instagram, Snapchat, and Twitter

viral: an image, video, or any other type of content that quickly grows in popularity and rapidly spreads throughout the internet and other media outlets

Social media sites help to connect people from all over the world. Websites like Facebook, Twitter, and Instagram are good examples of sites that allow us to get connected to our loved ones, no matter how far away they are from us.

Chapter Two
Social Media: Facebook, Instagram, Twitter, Etc. & Safety Online

Logging Online? So Are About 3.6 Billion Other People

Today, an estimated 49 percent of the world's population has access to the internet. This is compared to just 4 percent of the world's population back in 1999.

By February 2004, Facebook was born. The website literally changed the way people used the internet. Social media went from being a hobby to being an essential part of everyday life for everyone from kids to grandparents. Nowadays, websites like Instagram, Reddit, Twitter, Tumblr, Snapchat, and YouTube are places for people to meet, share news, share pictures, share videos, and share ideas on a daily basis.

Today's teens and tweens may find it hard to imagine living in a world without social media. In reality, many of your teachers, coaches, and other adults in your life didn't grow up with these outlets, or in some cases even with the Internet itself! The fact that such rapid growth and change has occurred in even just the last 20 years shows just how exciting the world of computer science and related fields can be.

Growing up with **social media**, however, can make it easy to take things for granted. We may not always be aware that the way we behave and interact with others on the Internet can have a negative impact.

How Too Much Social Media Can Be Stressful

Social media is a wonderful way to keep in touch with friends, spread ideas, and share special moments from your life. But like other aspects of the Internet, social media can be stressful if used too much.

Dos and Don'ts of Password and Username Safety

DO use a different password for every site

DO use an alias as your username if using chat room sites

DON'T make passwords too short

DON'T keep a password for too long

DON'T make a password that is easy to guess

DON'T use personal information in usernames or passwords

DON'T use your email address as a username

DON'T use real words. Use plenty of mixed characters

DON'T use passwords on computers you do not control

Social Media: Facebook, Instagram, Twitter, Etc. & Safety Online

One of the most important aspects of online etiquette is to **recognize when and if you are becoming dependent on your social media**. People who spend too much time online—even if they're talking to their friends—are more at risk of feeling depressed and socially isolated.

Ask yourself a few honest questions:
- Do you check your social media accounts a lot?
- Do you always use social media while you're doing other things like eating dinner, watching television, or doing homework?
- Do you find yourself often feeling down after looking at your friends' social media posts?
- Do you feel anxious if you don't have your phone with you, or if you haven't checked your social media in a while?

These may be signs of social media stress or burnout. Other signs can include withdrawing from friends and family, losing interest in activities you normally enjoy, spending hours and hours online, or having a hard time concentrating. This is actually a common experience for many kids and teenagers. It can affect your mood, concentration, schoolwork, and even your relationships with your friends and family.

If you notice any of these behaviors in yourself, know that you're not alone. Many people experience similar feelings. Try to improve the situation by having set breaks from social media. Reach out to a parent or another trusted adult and talk to them about how you've been feeling. They'll be able to help you figure out what to do next so that your social media outlets enhance your life rather than stress you out.

The Pros and Cons of Social Media

Be Social Media Savvy: Using Your Accounts Safely and Appropriately

There's no doubt that using social media can be a fun way to interact with your friends. But it's important to be smart about what information you share across all these different platforms, as anything you post, tweet, or snap can make a lasting impact on your life.

Take Snapchat, for instance. This popular **app** and website allows users to send photos, videos, and messages to their friends and followers. Snapchat is designed to automatically delete this content once it's been shared and viewed, or after a certain amount of time has passed (typically up to twenty-four hours).

However, this automatic delete action does not prevent other Snapchat users from capturing your photo, video, or message on their own phone or tablet. They can do this through a function on their device called a "screenshot," which allows a person to take a photo of what's currently displayed on their phone or tablet screen.

Instagram is similar. It even offers a "stories" option, much like Snapchat. While you can delete your Instagram photos after you've posted them, there's no way to stop your followers from saving the photos to their own phones before you do so.

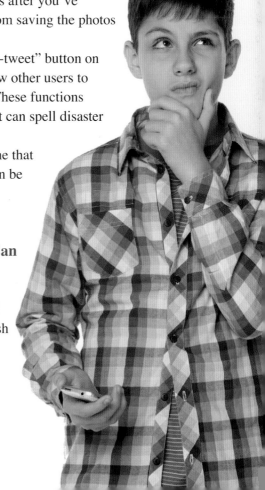

There are also "Regram" apps for Instagram, a "Re-tweet" button on Twitter, and a "Share" function on Facebook that allow other users to re-post your content directly through their accounts. These functions give life to **viral** videos and other popular content, but can spell disaster for you if you post something that you later regret.

So, what does this all mean for you? Simple: assume that everything you post on your social media accounts can be found and shared in a public sphere.

More than Just Embarrassing: A Risky Post Can Cost a Future

For this reason, sharing photos and videos of yourself or your friends doing illegal, dangerous, and/or foolish activities is a risk not worth taking. Publicly posting

Think carefully before posting online. If you wouldn't want your grandmother or teacher to see it, then don't post it!

Social Media: Facebook, Instagram, Twitter, Etc. & Safety Online

Even though some apps such as Snapchat delete images automatically after a fixed period of time, the person you shared them with may have saved or forwarded them.

about such behaviors (let alone engaging in them) can get you in trouble with a lot of different people.

Most businesses, for example, will search through prospective employees' social media accounts before going forward with a job application. It's a simple way to gauge a person's professionalism. By having inappropriate content on your social media accounts, you could end up being passed over for the job, no matter how good your résumé is.

Teens have even lost scholarships and have had their college acceptances rescinded after school admission officials have found inappropriate or incriminating photos of the students on their social media profiles.

Lastly, but perhaps most importantly, police and other law enforcement officers can use photos and videos shared on social media as evidence. This means that if you post about any underage drinking, drug use, truancy, or other inappropriate behaviors, you may be putting yourself at risk for investigation or even juvenile arrest.

Consider your social media accounts as your own digital billboards. They're like personal advertisements that can make a strong impression on others. Realize that the information you choose to share could boost (or ruin) your reputation, so share wisely.

Some Major Dos and Don'ts Of Social Media Etiquette

DO talk to your parents about the family rules for Internet use

DO like, comment on, and share your friends' posts, tweets, and blogs

DO say things online that you would be comfortable saying in person, too

DO follow public figures and people who inspire you with interesting and quality content

DO share tasteful photos of yourself and your daily life

DO keep your social media accounts marked as private to prevent strangers and scammers from looking at your content

DON'T use your social media as a personal diary

DON'T accept friend requests from people you don't know

DON'T use social media to share highly personal information, like your address, phone number, or birth date

DON'T share viral videos or content that is graphic or harmful in nature

DON'T share photos and videos of yourself and your friends engaging in illegal and/or inappropriate activities. If you are tagged in such content, DO tell your friend to remove the photo and/or flag the content as inappropriate

DON'T post too many selfies

Social Media: Facebook, Instagram, Twitter, Etc. & Safety Online

Social media is an excellent way to keep in touch with friends. Reading a nice message or hearing some interesting news can be a positive experience. However, too many incoming messages can sometimes be overwhelming, so try to limit your contacts to a manageble level.

Online Privacy: More Important Than a Perfect Selfie

It may seem obvious to you that sharing illegal, sexual, and other inappropriate content can have serious consequences for your future. But did you realize that even sharing your phone number via social media can be risky, too?

Unfortunately, sexual predators, scammers, and other nefarious characters are always lurking around online. They're looking for ways to take advantage of unsuspecting Internet users, and can even steal your or your parents' financial information. Being careless with what information you share on online can increase your risk of coming in contact with such people.

Private information should be kept private. This includes things like your age, phone number, date of birth, middle name, and address. When in doubt, ask your parents.

It's also worth noting that future employers and college admission offices often see "over-sharing" as an undesirable behavior from a potential employee or student. By maintaining your online privacy, you're protecting yourself and your family while also showing that you are a responsible person.

Text-Dependent Questions

1. What are some ways that you and your parents can help protect your online privacy?

2. Why would a prospective employer view an applicant's online social media?

3. Name three possible consequences of posting a photo of yourself at an underage drinking party.

Research Project

Interview an adult you know who grew up without a social media account like Facebook or Instagram. Even better, try to find an adult who didn't grow up with the Internet at all! Write a one-page essay that highlights their thoughts about social media, what it was like for them to learn how to use social media as an adult, if and/how social media has impacted their personal and professional relationships, and any other thoughts they may share.

Words to Understand

chain mail: a forwarded email that typically asks recipients to forward it along even further; chain mail often contains false information or a myth to try to elicit sympathy or fear

spam: irrelevant, unwanted, and/or inappropriate messages sent on the Internet to a large number of people

Writing an email should be carried out with the same care and attention as when writing a letter.

Chapter Three
Email Etiquette

It's hard to imagine living in a time when the only way to communicate with other people was through a landline phone or handwritten letters. But once fax machines, pagers, and cell phones came along, people quickly became used to the benefits of exchanging information extremely quickly and on a much wider scale.

These days, many of us seem to take for granted just how easy it is to communicate with others. For instance, you can send an email from New York that can be read almost immediately by a recipient in Japan. Or, instead of sending a letter, you can send a quick email to a friend in less time than it would have taken you to look for a stamp.

Having such a vast ability to communicate across the globe is a wonderful thing. But because email is so accessible and so easy to use, it's important to understand how to use it appropriately. While it may seem informal, email can still influence the impression you make on others, including your future bosses or academic leaders.

You've Got Mail
Email as we know it was first invented around the 1970s. Today, an estimated 205 billion emails are sent and received every day!

Four Rules for Sending the Perfect Email

It doesn't take long to write an email, and it doesn't take long to follow these four tips to ensure that your email is appropriate as well:

1. Use a Serious Email Address
Having a silly screen name to use with your friends may be fine. But these days, email is used as much for professional communication

Who Sent the First Email

The first email was sent by computer engineer Ray Tomlinson in 1971. The email was simply a test message to himself. It was sent from one computer to another computer sitting right beside it in Cambridge, Massachusetts, but it traveled via ARPANET, a network of computers that was the precursor to the Internet.

Email Etiquette

as it is for personal communication. Assume that at some point you'll have to send an email to a teacher, boss, or some other person whom you want to show respect to (and whom you want to be respected by). Would you want this person to read an email from you if your address was childish, offensive, or sexual in nature? Probably not.

Your email address can be as simple as your first and last name, or a variation using your initials or even a few numbers. You should ask your parents for their input when you create an email account. For privacy reasons, they may not want you to use your full name.

2. Check Your Grammar

No one is immune to grammar or spelling mistakes, so you need to get in the habit of rereading your emails before you send them in order to find and fix any obvious errors.

The more formal the message is (such as a note to a teacher), the more important it is that you use proper grammar, spelling, capitalization, and so on. Aside from presenting yourself in the best way possible, using good grammar also helps ensure that your intended message will be understood by the recipient.

WHY ARE YOU YELLING?

Typing in all capital letters has long been recognized as "yelling" on the Internet. Though you may think it can help get your point across, sentences written in all caps can be difficult to read and usually come off as rude. Avoid this altogether.

3. Check Your Formatting

By design, emails should be relatively short. Try to your keep your message to only two or three sentences per paragraph. Use a simple font that is twelve or fourteen point size. Don't use a distracting background.

If you're sending a formal email, then use a more formal, letter-type format. In your subject line, write a few words that describe the content of your email, such as "Questions About the Project" or "Responding to the Job Application." Keep in mind that if you are responding to a job listing online, many companies write specific instructions on what to write in the subject line and/or email itself. This is to help them sort out job applications by only looking at those sent by people who clearly read all the directions!

In the body of the email, begin with a polite introduction, such as "Hello, Mr. Smith," or "Dear Mrs. Smith." Do not use emojis, profanity, or abbreviations like "LOL" or "TTYL." Finish the email with a polite sign-off such as, "Sincerely, Tom."

Check your email inbox regularly and respond promptly, particulary to important emails.

Email Etiquette

It's not a good idea to send bad news via an email. There are times when a telephone call or meeting someone personally is the appropriate thing to do.

If you are responding to an email that is one of several in an exchange, consider removing the previous messages that are often automatically copied into the body of your email (this may vary depending on which email provider you use, such as Yahoo or Gmail, or even a school or company email). Having all these extra words can make your email look too busy or cluttered. You can always refer to older emails by checking your Sent folder or saving important emails in a separate folder.

4. Respond to Emails Promptly and Succinctly

Having good email etiquette is not just about writing politely and appropriately. It's also about responding to messages in a courteous way.

If a message requires a response, try to respond as soon as you can. Don't go days without replying. This is especially true for business- and academic-related messages.

Even sending a quick note just to acknowledge that you received the email is considerate and appreciative: "Just wanted to let you know that I got your message. I will get back to you as soon as I can."

Hoping for a quick response from someone? Instead of being pushy by closing with a statement like this, "Please respond ASAP," try a more polite approach: "Thank you for taking the time to read my message. I hope to hear from you soon."

If you are going on a family vacation or will be unable to access your email for a while, consider creating a "vacation response." You can set this up in a few simple steps by logging onto your email account and searching for the automatic response function (contact your email provider if you need help with this).

Three Emails You Should Never Send

Not all emails are created equal. There are plenty of times when sending an email may be considered inappropriate, cruel, or otherwise risky. Here are three types of emails you should avoid sending or forwarding altogether:

1. A Spam Email or "Chain Mail"

Spam emails are sent around the Internet by the billions every day. These often have inappropriate or outlandish subject lines. When you open a spam email, it may take you to another website, flood your inbox with more messages, or even install a virus onto your computer.

Chain emails (for example, "Send this to at least ten people in the next hour and your crush will fall in love with you") are also annoying to receive. These types of messages are like junk mail. Do not open or forward them.

2. An Email Sent When You're Angry

Once you send an email, you can't take it back. Firing off an angry message may feel satisfying in the moment, but chances are you'll regret it later once you've calmed down.

"Phishing"

Spam emails may appear to be from a financial institution, bank, or other well-known companies, such as Ebay, Amazon, etc. The emails usually ask that you reply or go to a website to confirm your account or bank card details. BEWARE: Reputable banks and companies never ask you to confirm information in this way. Although the email or website may look genuine, it is not. The scammers will take your details and often use them for illegal purposes, such as identity theft or credit card fraud. This type of scam is called "Phishing," and is common, so be prepared.

NEVER give out personal information such as bank or credit card details by email, or in response to an email, without first checking with the company the email "appears" to be from.

If you are at all unsure, ALWAYS contact the bank or company through methods you trust (such as calling your bank) to confirm that they sent you the email.

Email Etiquette

If you are upset, angry, or feeling any other strong emotion, that is not a good time to write an email. Instead, try drafting an email or even write down a letter by hand to the person you're upset with—but do not send it. This can actually help you work through your emotions in the moment, plus you'll avoid saying something mean or hurtful.

Later on, once you've calmed down (whether a few hours or a few days later), feel free to share your feelings with this person. Whether you decide to do that through email or another method is up to you . . . See the next point.

3. An Email That Should Probably Be a Phone Call or Face-To-Face Conversation Instead

Sometimes, it may seem better to say something difficult in an email, since it can be awkward to have tough conversations in person. But no matter how formal your email is, some subjects shouldn't be discussed using this type of communication.

Use your best judgment here. If the matter is urgent, extremely personal, or involves a lot of private information, then don't send it as an email. Call or speak directly with the person instead.

In a formal environment, such as at work, an email is a great form of communication that will ensure your message arrives at the desk of the person you need to correspond with.

A Word on Instant Messaging, Direct Messaging, and Texting

Email continues to be used a lot within the professional and personal realms of online communication. In fact, as much as a third of the world's population is expected to be using email by the end of 2019. However, within the past several years, other forms of online communication have exploded in popularity, including instant messaging, direct messaging on social media apps, and texting.

In general, texts and instant messages are much more informal compared to emails. That said, you still shouldn't fire off a text or message when you are upset. Also make sure that the content you're sharing isn't graphic, sexual, or inappropriate in nature. At best, this could cause someone to feel uncomfortable or hurt. At worst, it could cost you a friendship or even get you in trouble with your school or local law enforcement (for example, if you send sexually explicit photos of yourself or others who are underage).

Text-Dependent Questions

1. Should you include smiley faces and abbreviations in an email sent to a boss or college administration official?

2. You're going on vacation with your family for a week and won't be able to log on to your email. What can you do to make sure people know that you're unable to respond to your emails and that you're not simply ignoring them?

3. How much of the world's population is expected to be using email by the year 2019?

Research Project

Using the information laid out in this chapter, send an email to your principal or teacher. Consider asking them to give you feedback on what they thought about your message and how they think you could improve—your future boss will appreciate it!

Words to Understand

cyberbullying: the persistent and mean-spirited use of digital-communication tools to make another person feel angry, sad, or scared

trolling: posting a deliberately offensive or provocative online post with the aim of upsetting someone or eliciting an angry response from them

While girls are more likely to be the subject of online bullying, they can also be the perpetrators.

Chapter Four
Respect for Others Online

We all want to feel free to enjoy the Internet without fearing that we will be ridiculed, shamed, or put down. Unfortunately, we can't control anyone else's behaviors, thoughts, or words. This means that if we're going to use the Internet, we have to face the possibility that some people may take this as an opportunity to try to hurt our feelings.

Why is this so prevalent? It could be that as a society, we are spending more and more time online. Such a large proportion of our interactions with other people is through social media, YouTube, email, and other platforms within the digital world. It makes sense then that the more time we spend interacting with others online, the more likely it is that we're going to come in contact with people who want to do or say hurtful things.

Sugar and Spice and Everything Nice?
Research shows that girls are twice as likely as boys to be victims of cyberbullying. However, girls are also twice as likely to be the ones doing the cyberbullying, too.

Another reason why online **trolling** and bullying are relatively common is that it's much easier to hide behind a keyboard and write a mean comment than it is to say the comment directly to a person's face. In fact, most people who leave mean comments or send hurtful messages would never be willing to say the same things in person. The illusion of anonymity makes people feel as though they can say anything online because they think they're safe from real-world consequences. Unfortunately, this can make them think that saying intentionally rude, offensive, or disrespectful things isn't a big deal.

Cyberbullying is cruel and can cause long-term damage to the victim.

Respect for Others Online

In reality, it can be a big deal. Words really do hurt, whether they are spoken or written. Perhaps more than anything else, having good online etiquette is about ensuring that you use your words wisely and treat other people on the Internet with as much respect and decency as possible.

It Starts with You: Five Ways to Start Being More Respectful Online

1. Think Before You Post

It's simple: be considerate about the things you say. You should never use the Internet to put down other people or make people feel badly about themselves. It may feel like you're invisible when commenting on someone's video, post, or wall, especially if it's from a person you don't know. But a real person with real feelings will read your comment, and if you didn't think carefully about what you said then your message could come off as very hurtful.

It's worth remembering, too, that a history of poor etiquette online may also come back to haunt you in the future, especially when it comes to college or job applications.

Treat your friends and acquaintances with respect when using social media. This will make the whole experience fun and rewarding.

Even if you delete an unkind text, tweet, Snapchat, Facebook post, or video, there's no guarantee that someone else didn't already get a chance to save it themselves or forward it to someone else.

2. If It's Intentionally Hurtful, Don't Share It

Don't share content that is obviously meant to embarrass, ridicule, or hurt other people. If a friend shares such content with you, feel free to tell them privately that you're not interested in seeing that kind of stuff. This may be enough to help your friend realize that they're acting disrespectfully and inspire them to change their own behavior.

3. Agree to Disagree

You don't have to share the same opinions with everyone you engage with online. In fact, it's a good thing to expose yourself to different ideas, perspectives, and world views. That said, if someone says something you disagree with, feel free to state your opinion, but be respectful of theirs. If the other person begins to speak in disparaging or hurtful ways, then it's better to quietly remove yourself from the conversation than to try to reason with them or engage with them further.

4. Honor Another Person's Digital Space

Avoid sending long messages, multiple emails, or too many text messages at once to someone. This can come off as clingy and irritating, and it is also not a good way to respect a person's right to privacy and personal space.

5. Support Your Friends Who Are Being Trolled or Bullied Online

Research shows that if your friends stand up to your cyberbullies you'll be better able to handle the challenges of being targeted. Bullies tend to seek out people they perceive as vulnerable targets, so having a group of friends rallying around you can be a powerful way to take away some of the bully's power.

Cyberbullying IS Bullying!

Around 30–40 percent of teens say they've been bullied online, and over eighty percent of teens believe that online bullying is easier to get away with than bullying that happens face-to-face. But even if it doesn't seem like a big deal, cyberbullying can lead to significant mental and emotional distress, low self-esteem, self-harm, anxiety, and physical illness—just like bullying done in person. For more information, go to www.stopbullying.gov

Respect for Others Online

You can support your friends by letting them know you care about them and that you're here for them if they want to talk. You can also show your support by sharing positive images, videos, stories, and messages through social media and email to help combat a lot of the negativity that's easily found online.

I Didn't Mean It Like That! What To Do When You Goof Up Online

Have you ever said something to someone out of anger or frustration, but then regretted it later and apologized? Have you ever said something that you later realized was misinterpreted as cruel or ignorant? This doesn't necessarily make you a bully or a bad person. Instead, it serves as a reminder that words have real-world consequences online—whether you intend them or not.

In the same vein, disrespect toward another person online isn't always intentional, nor does it always constitute cyberbullying. Sometimes, you may simply not handle your emotions well in the moment and therefore say something hurtful as a result of that. Or, instead of carefully thinking out your response to someone, you may send a message that

If you are bullied online, don't hesitate to tell a parent, teacher, or friend.

A Thought-Provoking Video about Cyberbullying.

comes off as flip, rude, or some other form of disrespect—even if this wasn't your intent.

This isn't an excuse for impolite behavior or words, of course. If you do say something out of anger toward someone else online, think about what you could have done/said differently, think about the impact your words had on the other person and consider speaking to the other person face-to-face about what happened.

Handling The "Haters": What To Do If You're Being Trolled or Bullied

Aside from doing your part to spread positivity online, having good online etiquette can also help protect yourself from the negativity spread by bullies and trolls. This is important because if you want to enjoy the Internet, then you need to realize it's impossible to completely avoid people who are unkind.

Instead, it's wiser to learn strategies that can help you respond (or not respond) to haters more effectively. This gives you better peace of mind and leaves you free to use the Internet without completely losing your self-confidence.

The next time you're dealing with someone being rude to you online, try any one of the following tactics. Figure out which ones help you most in different situations:

1. Don't Respond

People who leave trolling comments are just looking to start arguments and get a reaction out of you. By giving no reaction to them whatsoever, you're reducing their power by not giving them what they want. If someone sends you a mean message, just delete it and ignore it.

2. Talk or Write About Your Feelings

It doesn't feel good to be mistreated. When you need a shoulder to lean on, speak to people you can trust and talk to them about your experience. If the comments are threatening, violent, persistent, or otherwise making you feel unsafe, you do need to talk to your parents. Your school or law enforcement may also need to get involved.

Interestingly, only about one in ten kids who have experienced online bullying will tell a trusted adult about it. If you don't feel comfortable talking to your parent, then tell a close friend or sibling instead. Even writing about your feelings in a journal can help you work through your emotions more quickly and ease some of your pain and sadness.

3. Understand That It's Not Really About You

None of us is perfect. We all have doubts and judgments about ourselves. If we see someone who stirs up those insecure feelings we have within ourselves, then we may become tempted to lash out at them.

If someone is bullying or trolling you online, don't retaliate — you will just fuel the fire. Instead, "block" the individual, turn your device off, and do something else with "real" friends.

If someone says something rude to you online, try to realize that this person is most likely just projecting his or her own self-doubt, frustration, and anger onto you. It's still okay to be temporarily upset by what was said, especially if it was said with a clear intention to hurt you. But by remembering that their reasons for saying these things were not really about you, it will be easier to let it roll off your shoulders and stop yourself taking it too personally.

4. Block or Log Off

Many social media apps like Facebook and Instagram allow you to block users. This prevents them from being able to look at your page or send you messages.

Consider blocking someone if they have a history of being rude to you or other people you know. In addition to blocking someone, you can also try logging off and stepping away from your phone or computer for a while. Do something offline that you love to do, like read, draw, or play sports. Do something to get your mind off of the disrespectful comments and help prevent yourself from saying something back to them that you may later regret.

Text-Dependent Questions

1. According to research, which group is more likely to be both the victims and perpetrators of cyberbullying: boys or girls?

2. Approximately what percentage of kids and teens have experienced online bullying?

3. List three things that you can do to help yourself the next time someone posts a mean comment about you online.

Research Project

Do some research on the effects of bullying (including cyber bullying). These effects can be mental, emotional, social, or even physical. Write a two-page report about your findings, and discuss some ways that kids can learn how to handle being bullied in a more effective and empowering way.

Words to Understand

media literate: being able to access, analyze, evaluate, create, and participate in communication channels in a variety of forms, including print, video, and online

misinformation: false or inaccurate information that is either unintentional (shared without realizing it is untrue) or deliberately deceptive

skeptical: to be inclined to question or doubt commonly accepted opinions and ideas

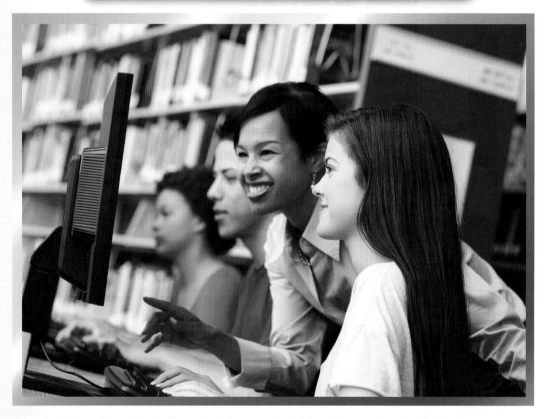

Accessing information online is a fast and efficient way in which students can broaden their horizons.

Chapter Five
Internet Resources & Keeping Pace With Current Affairs

"Don't believe everything you read on the Internet." —Abraham Lincoln

The above quotation is a humorous reminder that just because you read something on the Internet doesn't mean it's true. This is important to remember, because we use the Internet every day to learn, make decisions, and stay up-to-date on current affairs that affect the world we live in.

Good online etiquette requires that you use a little healthy discretion when it comes to reading and citing websites. If we want to avoid relying on or spreading **misinformation**, we must learn how to identify quality online sources and weed out the bad ones that may be poorly researched at best, or blatantly deceptive at worst.

Tips for Improving and Organizing Your Research

Developing good online research habits now will be of great use to you when you're older. As a young adult, you'll need to use the Internet to help you with more advanced academic studies if you go to college or university. You'll also be using the Internet to help you make important life decisions about things like financial investments, charitable donations, major purchases like a car or a home, and voting.

Having good research habits can improve your academic performance and enhance your overall understanding of a given subject.

Search engines, such as Google, can be used to research a specific topic.

It is smart thinking to structure your research by making detailed notes before you begin work online.

The following are some helpful tips to aid with your research, no matter what topic you may be investigating:

1. Use High-Quality or Official Websites for Your Research

Whenever possible, look for articles and data that come from well-respected sources. Why? Such sources are more likely to have accurate information presented in an unbiased way, and use data that are either peer-reviewed or supported by scientific evidence.

Generally acceptable resources include national organizations, governmental websites, and universities. Sites that end in .edu or .org also tend to be more credible.

Avoid relying solely on news and information from Wikipedia, social media, podcasts, and blogs. These sites can sometimes share good information, but they are more likely to present misinformation, so make sure all your research is corroborated.

A Free Website For Kid-Friendly News

The website https://newsela.com helps students learn about a wide range of topics. It's free to open an account, which gives you access to thousands of articles written at a variety of reading levels.

Additional sites like YouTube and TED are often full of interesting information, but you should still utilize several different sources to bolster your research.

2. Use Tools and Apps to Help You Organize Your Research Notes

Depending on the amount of research you have to do, it can be easy to get overwhelmed by all the information you find. Plus, in our fast-paced world, breaking news happens all the time and things can change quickly. There are a number of helpful tools out there to help you stay on top of everything and make sense of what you're learning:

- Google Docs allows you to create and save documents securely online; you can even share the document with classmates who are working on a project with you for simple collaboration.
- Google Alerts notifies you when new content about your topic comes out online, helping you stay up-to-date as you complete your project.
- The website InstaGrok allows you look up any topic and then use an interactive concept map to see and share information, without being too text-heavy.

There are various online organizers you can use, such as Google Docs, where you can store website information.

Nowadays, we are constantly bombarded with news stories on social media. Make sure that you verify a story elsewhere before believing it.

3. Be a Healthy Skeptic of All News

Sometimes people share fake news unwittingly. They may not realize that the facts they are reporting are not based on accurate or valid scientific research. Other people may share fake news on purpose in an attempt to sway readers' opinions for political or economic gain.

In either case, using the most credible resources you can find can help you avoid false news. But even many well-known websites and news outlets have been shown to be biased or report misinformation at times.

One of your jobs as a student is to learn how to be **skeptical** about what you see on the Internet, especially on your social media feeds where you spend a lot of your time.

When you see a news headline, instead of just believing what it says, ask yourself some helpful and healthy skeptical questions from Project Look Sharp:

- Who made this content?
- Who paid for this content? Or, who gets paid if you click on this?
- Is this credible (and what makes you think that)?
- Who might benefit or be harmed by this message?
- What is left out of this message that might be important?

Asking the right questions about the online sources you find helps you become more **media literate**. So, feel free to use the news to support your research, but be aware that many of the most popular news sites and stations have a particular political bias one way or the other. Your goal shouldn't be to avoid the news, but rather to ask the right questions about what you see, hear, and read so you can learn to think for yourself.

4. Don't Rely Purely on the Internet for Resources
In this case, good online etiquette means knowing when to go offline, too. Though the Internet can give you access to a good amount of information, your school or local library can also provide good and trustworthy resources for almost any topic you're researching.

Don't automatically believe everything you read. Anyone can post information online. Always double-check any facts using other websites, or more traditional resources, such as books or magazines.

Extra, Extra! . . . Don't Read All About It!

Look for educational books, especially ones written by top professionals in a given field. You can ask your librarian to help you find additional resources that you might not find on your own. Your school or local library may also be able to help you access peer-reviewed journals and other publications so you can look at scientific studies that have been published about your topic.

Don't just rely wholly on the internet for research. Libraries are also excellent sources of information — and don't forget the librarian, who can advise you on good sources for study.

Helpful Fact-Checking Websites for Kids and Teens

Fact-checking is a way to make sure that information shared in news articles and other sources is accurate. When doing research for a school project, consider checking out any one of these quality fact-checking and news websites:

- Poynter.org
- OpenSecrets.org
- Snopes.com
- FactCheck.org

Using these resources helps to ensure that the information you're including in your report is as accurate and as truthful as possible. You can use these websites easily by entering keywords into the search bar on each site.

Text-Dependent Questions

1. What are three ways to spot a fake news story? Return to this video for helpful hints: https://www.commonsensemedia.org/blog/how-to-spot-fake-news-and-teach-kids-to-be-media-savvy.

2. What does it mean to be media literate? What kind of questions does a media-literate student ask while reading a news article?

3. Why is it important to develop good online research habits when you're young?

Research Project

Research a current "hot-button" issue in the news that interests you, like immigration or climate change. Be sure to use some of the fact-checking websites listed above to help support your research. Then, write a brief one-page report covering the key points of the issue, summarizing the main "for" and "against" points of view.

Words to Understand

authentic: Accurate representation of the facts

profiles: Biographical accounts presenting peoples' noteworthy characteristics and achievements

self-promotion: promoting or publicizing oneself or one's activities

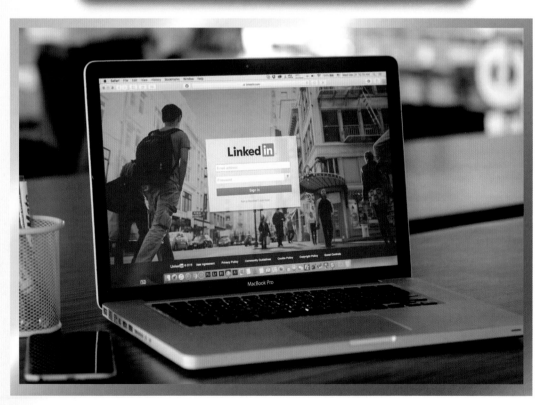

Business networking sites such as LinkedIn are excellent ways of promoting yourself.

Chapter Six
Self-Promotion, LinkedIn
& Other Business Networks

As a student, you may not think a lot about promoting yourself. But eventually, you'll graduate high school and head out to college or the professional world. By the time this happens, you'll want to have established a good reputation for yourself online.

Why? Employers and higher education officials often learn about potential hires or future students by checking out their social media **profiles**. They can look at the content you share, the way you engage with others, and the way you present yourself to assess qualities like professionalism, responsibility, integrity, kindness, generosity, and other things that matter to businesses and universities.

In a way, you're always promoting yourself online, whether you realize it or not. Good online etiquette is about making sure that you're promoting the best, most **authentic** version of yourself at all times. This helps you make a good impression on anyone who may be looking to learn more about you.

Polite and Professional Ways to Promote Yourself Online

There are many ways you can use your online presence to help you achieve your goals as a student and someday as a recent grad looking to start new career. Remember, everything you do online can be considered a form of **self-promotion**, from the comments you post to the videos you share and the links you forward, so be sure that what you are doing promotes yourself in a positive way.

When presenting yourself online, you need to show the "true you." Show quality images of yourself smartly dressed.

Self-Promotion, LinkedIn & Other Business Networks

Creating an eye-catching profile page is very important. Use quality images and provide relevant information about yourself in a clear and concise manner.

Use High-Quality Photos on All Your Social Media Pages

Think about your social media profiles as advertisements for yourself. To put your best face forward (literally), always use appropriate photos on your profile. Your photo should be flattering, high-quality, and clearly show your face. Avoid using screen grabs or pixelated images. Pose and dress tastefully, and avoid having other people in your photo. Since your photo is usually one of the first things people notice, it can have a big impact on the first impression you make. The more professional-looking the photo, the easier it will be for other people to take you seriously.

Create an Account on LinkedIn or Other Business Networks

Social media connects you with your friends and the rest of the world. It also can also help you advance your career and open up professional opportunities when you're older.

One of the most popular social media networks used by business professionals is LinkedIn. It's similar to Facebook, but designed specifically to help people share and connect with colleagues, professionals, employers, employees, and business partners. You can customize your profile to showcase your accomplishments, education, awards, and membership of professional organizations. If you're good at certain things, like Microsoft Excel or PowerPoint, you can also highlight these skills.

If you're new to the workforce or about to enter it, you can use LinkedIn to help you find a job or internship. The site is also a great way to network with other people who can help you learn more about the field you're interested in.

Businesses and employers use LinkedIn to help find potential employees who may be a good fit for their company. It's also a great way for them to market themselves and get people interested in their products and services.

That's a Whole Lot of Linking Going On
LinkedIn was founded in 2003 by a team led by entrepreneur Reid Hoffman. Since then, the social network has expanded to around 500 million users from over 200 countries!

Consider Starting a Blog
With your parent's permission and help, you may want to launch your own personal website. This is a great place to share your own opinions, thoughts, creative work, and projects you're involved in. If you have a special interest or hobby, you can dedicate your blog to this topic.

A personal website can also act as a great way to raise awareness about a cause that you care about. You can help readers of your blog learn more about the cause and how to contribute by directing them to organizations and fundraisers.

There are two main ways to run a blog: a free blog or a self-hosted blog. If you choose to launch a free blog, keep in mind that your web address will have to be "shared" with whatever blogging platform you're using. For instance, if you're using WordPress.com, then your address will look like this: myfirstblog.wordpress.com. With a free blog, you also do not necessarily own any of the content, or even the blog itself.

Some of the most popular free blog platforms include WordPress.com, Blogger.com, Tumblr.com, Weebly.com, and Medium.com.

All Over the Web
WordPress is a blogging and website content managing system (CMS) that currently powers at least 25 percent of the Internet.

A self-hosted blog gives you more control and freedom over your website. You have to pay to create and maintain one; however, you'll have full ownership over all the content you post. If you plan on keeping your blog for a long time or potentially using it someday to provide income, this may be a good option.

Apply Smart, Apply Safe: Tips for Doing Online Job Searches

When you're old enough to start working, applying for work can be a daunting process. Getting a job that interests you and pays you a decent wage can be challenging. Fortunately, the Internet is now a major resource that can help with your search. With adult supervision, teens and young adults can use online resources to do everything from network with potential employers, secure internship opportunities, upload and share a résumé, and fill out online job applications.

Skype and Facetime are two websites that make it possible to have an interview online. This method is often used by employment agencies to interview candidates.

Applying for a job online is an easy and efficient way of getting your application in on time.

Finding Work in the Digital Age

According to data from the Pew Research Center, 79 percent of Americans looking for work in the past few years have used the Internet to help them. 34 percent report that the Internet was the most important tool they used.

If you decide to use the Internet to help you find a job, whether now or later on in your academic and professional careers, consider the following tips:

Use Legitimate Online Job Sites

Some of the best job searching sites, in addition to LinkedIn, are:

- Monster.com
- Indeed.com
- CareerBuilder.com
- GlassDoor.com
- Nexxt.com
- Gadball.com
- SimplyHired.com

Once you have been offered an interview as the result of an online application, it is important to turn up smartly dressed and well-prepared for the task ahead.

You can even do a Google search to find job sites that are specifically geared toward certain careers, like engineering or health care.

A word of caution: be wary when applying for jobs on sites like Craigslist. Ask your parents for help to ensure that you're responding to legitimate companies. Scammers have been known to use Craigslist and similar websites to steal private information or money from unsuspecting respondents. If a job listing asks for things like payment information or your social security number, stay away.

Read the Job Description Carefully

When looking at a job description, consider what the employer or company is asking for. Do you have the necessary skills and experience? Are you able to commit to the number of hours that the employer is asking for? Respect the employer's time by only responding to a job application if you are seriously interested in the job. Chances are, there will be several other people applying for the same position. Do your part to stand out in a competitive environment by being polite and gracious.

Some companies and employers will post specific instructions about how to apply in their job listings, such as writing a certain phrase in the subject line. This is to make sure that you've read the listing thoroughly and shows that you are attentive and responsible.

Practice Good Email Etiquette

The earlier chapter on using email will help you respond professionally to an online job posting. If you have any questions about the job role, an email can be a good place to seek clarification and show that you have serious interest in the job. Being timely with your response to potential employers is extremely important as they will likely be fielding many other emails from potential hires.

As a teen or young adult, you may not have a lot of professional experience. This is why self-promotion online, either through your social media sites or even a personal blog, can be a helpful way to bolster your chances of getting an interview.

Text-Dependent Questions

1. About how many people use the social networking site LinkedIn?

2. Name three credible websites where you can search for jobs online.

3. In recent years, what percentage of Americans have used the Internet to look for a job?

Research Project

Visit one of the free online job sites listed in the chapter. Spend ten to fifteen minutes searching through available jobs in a field that you may be interested in. Write down a list of the common skills, experiences, and characteristics that a job in this field requires, then write a one-page essay on ways you could work toward developing those skills and experiences while still a student.

Words to Understand

digital citizen: a person who uses technology to engage in society, politics, and government; people who use the Internet regularly and effectively

follower: a user who chooses to see all of another user's posts in their content feed

netiquette: the correct or acceptable way of communicating on the Internet

Social media can be accessed via a cell phone anywhere and at any time of day.

Chapter Seven
Keeping & Making Good Contacts Online

In this book, you've learned about ways to improve your **netiquette** on the web. From interacting with others in a safe and respectful way, to finding and using credible online sources for schoolwork and career opportunities, to making a good first impression, good Internet etiquette can have a positive impact on virtually everything you do online and offline, too.

Perhaps one of the most beneficial things about learning how to use the Internet safely and respectfully is that it can help you connect with people from all over the world. These are people you may never have had the chance to interact with otherwise.

Other students, mentors, teachers, and leaders of small businesses and charitable organizations are all people you may want to get to know and communicate with. Such connections may help you someday land a job, join a start-up company, contribute to a movement, or even earn money.

Tips for Making Good Connections Online

The connection you make with another person or a group of people online can be extremely rewarding and valuable, both personally and professionally. You can maintain these connections by practicing good Internet etiquette, as well as using some of the following tips:

Follow Inspirational People on Social Media
Many world leaders, professional athletes, writers, and other celebrities use social media.

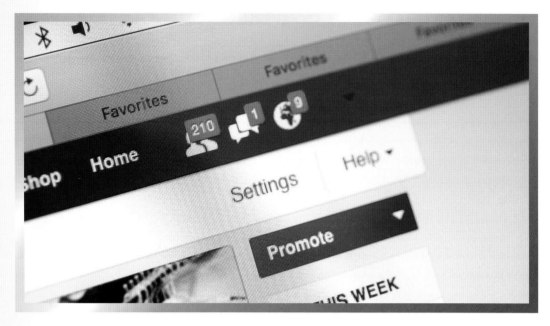

It is common for teenagers today to accept and collect as many friends on social media as possible. Think carefully before adding someone to your social media. Are they nice, influential, or interesting, and most importantly, do you know them?

By following those who are good role models, you can find other fans who share similar ideas and values as you do.

Of course, a person doesn't have to be famous to be inspirational. Search Instagram, Snapchat, Facebook, and other social media networks to find everyday people who are sharing positive, empowering, and interesting content on a regular basis. Chances are, if you find their pages interesting, other people will, too.

In this context, being a **follower** isn't a bad thing. You can help the people you follow on social media by letting them know about other content, such as books, blogs, and movies, that relate to your common interests and which expand your knowledge about the subject.

Sign Up for Online Groups and Organizations Related to Your Hobbies and Interests

Help people find you by interacting with online groups and forums that are related to areas you're interested in. This can include Facebook groups, LinkedIn, local and national groups, and professional organizations. Consider that colleges and universities like to see participation in activities outside of school. It shows that you are a well-rounded person with many interests and unique skills.

Ask your parents, teachers, or librarians for help finding credible and safe online communities to join. For privacy reasons, your parents may ask you to not use your real name.

Safety First, Always

Remember, you should never share your personal contact information with people you meet online without first talking to your parents about it.

If used properly and with respect, being online can offer a wealth of opportunities to make new friends, gain knowledge, and help with a future career.

Keeping & Making Good Contacts Online

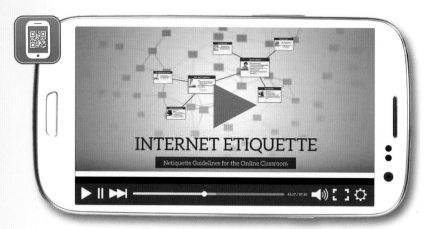

**Internet Etiquette:
For the Online
Classroom**

If you discover some very interesting content online, it is great to share what you've found with friends.

Contribute Meaningfully to the Conversation

Read, comment on, and share content posted by other people on social media or by members of an online community. Make sure that any comments you make demonstrate good etiquette. Doing so shows that you are being a responsible **digital citizen** by interacting appropriately and effectively with others.

This means your comments should be thoughtful and respectful. Ideally, your comments will inspire others to join in on the conversation.

Don't just post a comment simply to get noticed. Write something that genuinely contributes to the discussion. If you have a unique perspective or special knowledge about a certain topic, let others know. If others see you engaging in a considerate way, they may be more interested in getting to know you.

The internet is a big place. Standing out, staying safe, and being kind and considerate online are all part of your responsibilities as a young person in the digital age. Commit yourself to developing good online habits now so that you can make a powerful and positive impact on your academic, professional, and personal future.

Text-Dependent Questions

1. What is a digital citizen?

2. If another person on social media asks for your email address or phone number, what should you do?

3. What is the Golden Rule of online etiquette?

Research Project

Write an essay about five inspirational people you have read about on the Internet.

Series Glossary of Key Terms

appreciation	Gratitude and thankful recognition.
body language	Nonverbal communication through posture or facial expression.
bully	Overbearing person who habitually intimidates weaker or smaller people.
civil	Adhering to the norms of polite social intercourse.
clingy	Tending to stay very close to someone for emotional support.
common sense	Sound judgment based on simple perceptions of a situation.
compatible	Capable of existing together in harmony.
compliment	An expression of affection, respect, or admiration.
confidence	The state of being certain.
cyberbullying	The electronic posting of mean-spirited messages about a person.
empathy	Being aware of the feelings and thoughts of another.
eulogy	A commendatory oration or writing, especially in honor of one deceased.
faux pas	A social blunder.
frenemy	One who pretends to be a friend but is actually an emeny.
gossip	A person who habitually reveals personal facts about others.
grace	Disposition to act with kindness and courtesy.
inappropriate	Not suited for a purpose or situation.
initiative	The power to do something before others do.
inoculation	Injecting a vaccine to protect against or treat disease.
integrity	The quality of being honest and fair.
judgmental	Tending to judge people too quickly and critically.
lust	To have an intense desire or need.
manner	The way something is done or happens.
networking	The cultivation of productive relationships.
peer	One who is of equal standing with another.
poise	A natural, self-confident manner.
polite	Having or showing good manners or respect for others.
prioritize	To organize things so that the most important one is dealt with first.
procrastinate	To put off intentionally and habitually.
problem-solving	The process of finding a solution to a problem.
online	Connected to a computer.
relationship	The way in which two or more people are connected.
respect	To consider worthy of high regard.
RSVP	To respond to an invitation.
self-centered	Concerned solely with one's own needs.
socialize	Partcipate in social activities.
social media	Forms of electronic communications through which users share information, ideas, and personal messages.
staying power	Capacity of continuing without weakening.
sympathy	Caring about someone else's misfortune or grief.
tact	A keen sense of what to do or say without upsetting other people.

Further Reading

Patchin, Justin W., and Sameer Hinduja. *Words Wound: Delete Cyberbullying and Make Kindness Go Viral*. Minneapolis, MN: Free Spirit Publishing, 2014.

Sadleir, Emma, and Lizzie Harrison. *Selfies, Sexts and Smartphones: A Teenager's Online Survival Guide*. Cape Town: Penguin Books, 2017.

Lomeli, Roland. *Netiquette: A Guide to Etiquette in an Online World*. Anaheim, CA: BuzzTrace Publications, 2017.

Internet Resources

www.commonsensemedia.org This is a nonprofit organization based in San Francisco. The company provides education for kids and families about improving media and technology safety.

www.dosomething.org Join 5.5 million other American youths and get involved with social change. Choose from thousands of campaigns that cover everything from building self-esteem to fighting bullying.

www.hoopladigital.com Free access to thousands of audiobooks, music, videos, and ebooks. This website is like having your free public library everywhere you go, right at your fingertips.

www.internetassociation.org The mission of this website is to promote policies that protect the future of the Internet. Click here for current news that affects the online world, including trade, net neutrality, the sharing economy, and more.

www.safekids.com This is one of the oldest websites promoting internet safety. It offers safety advice, guides, and more for kids, teens, and parents. The website is founded by Larry Magid, who also the president and CEO of ConnectSafely.org.

Publisher's note:
The websites listed on this page were active at the time of publication. The publisher is not responsible for websites that have changed their addresses or discontinued operation since the date of publication. The publisher will review and update the website list upon each reprint.

Index

A

Access to Internet, 15
Anonymity, 31

B

Blocking, 37
Blog, 49–50
Breaks from social media, 16
Bullying, 30. *See also* Cyberbullying
Burnout, 16
Business networks, 48–49

C

Capital letters, 24
College, 18, 21
Commenting, 59
Common Sense Media, 9
Communication, nonverbal, 9
Connections to others, 14
Contacts, 55–59
  adding, 56
  follow inspirational people, 55–56
  making good connections online, 55–56
Content managing system (CMS), 49
Contributing online, 59
Craigslist, 52
Cyberbullying, 11, 31–32
  blocking or logging off, 37
  don't respond, 35
  it isn't about you, 36–37

statistics, 33
talk about your experience, 36
what to do, 35–37

D

Dangers of online posts, 17–19
Dependency on social media, 16
Digital
  citizen, 59
  footprint, 12, 13
Direct messaging, 29

E

Email, 11, 22, 23–29
  address, choosing, 23–24
  and bad news, 25
  body, 25
  chain mail, 27
  checking, 25
  font, 25
  formatting, 25
  grammar, 24
  instead of other communication, 28
  invention of, 23
  paragraphs, 25
  respond promptly, 26–27
  spam, 27
  string, 26
  subject line, 25
  types not to send, 27–28
  volume of, 29
  when angry, 27–28
Emojis, 25

Employers, 18, 21, 47, 48–49
Etiquette
  defined, 10
  dos and don'ts, 19
  importance of, 9–13
Evidence, 19

F

Facebook, 9, 10, 14, 15, 37
  sharing, 17
Facetime, 50
Fact-checking websites, 45
FactCheck.org, 45
Followers, 56
Friend requests, 19
Friends, staying in touch with, 20

G

Golden Rule, 9
Google Alerts, 41
Google Docs, 41
Groups online, 56–57

H

Harassment, 11
Hoffman, Reid, 49

I

Illegal activities, 19
Instagram, 9, 10, 14, 15, 37
  Regram, 17
  stories, 17
InstaGrok, 41
Instant messaging, 29
Internet research, 39–44
  high-quality or official

Picture Credits

All images in this book are in the public domain or have been supplied under license by © Shutterstock.com. To the best knowledge of the publisher, all images not specifically credited are in the public domain. If any image has been inadvertently uncredited, please notify the publisher, so that credit can be given in future printings.

Video Credits

Page 16 NBC News/Jack Murnin: http://x-qr.net/1Hpt, page 24 SDSU Continuing & Distance Education: http://x-qr.net/1FV2, page 35 PSA Web Video produced through STRUTT: http://x-qr.net/1GAZ, page 44 Commonsense Media: http://x-qr.net/1EQ3, page 58 Tracey Brown: http://x-qr.net/1Gmb

About the Author

Sarah Smith is a freelance writer currently living and working in the Boston area. She is also a board-certified Doctor of Physical Therapy, licensed by the Commonwealth of Massachusetts. She attended Boston University, where she earned both her doctorate and, as an undergraduate, a bachelor of science in health studies.

Sarah has been writing for her entire life, and first became a published author at age fourteen, when she began contributing to a weekly column for her local newspaper. Since beginning her freelance writing career in earnest in 2014, Sarah has written over 1,500 articles and books. Her work covers a broad range of topics, including psychology and relationships, as well as physical and mental health.

Additionally, she has over fifteen years of professional experience working with typically developing and special-needs children, along with their families, in a variety of settings, including schools, pediatric hospitals, and youth-group fitness programs. She spent over thirteen years working as a private nanny and babysitter for families in both her hometown of Yarmouth, Maine, as well as in and around the great city of Boston. Sarah also has experience tutoring and leading teens and young adults as part of a variety of clinical internship programs for physical therapy.